THE HONORING LIFE

Tiffany Graham

ISBN (Paperback): 979-8-9886154-8-4
ISBN (eBook): 979-8-9886154-7-7

Dedication

For my children: Kinsley, Harper, and Grayson.
I pray you learn the meaning of honor through our words and deeds. May God cover all that we miss.
I love you so much!

Acknowledgments

This book is dedicated to my parents. I didn't get it right growing up but I'm doing my best now. Thank you for doing what you could with what you had. I love you and am grateful for you both.

To my husband. Thank you for being an example of honor for me and our children. You have walked uprightly, righteously, for as long as I have known you. You challenge me and encourage me to be and do my best. I never understood your lack of offense or how you could just breeze through certain situations. You're easy going, loving, calm and collected. I'm full of passion, zeal, and an advocate for justice. You showed me, with some tough love, that honor is the way to go, and I don't have to fight everyone's battles. I love you for that and I'm grateful that the Lord used you as a conduit to jumpstart this revelation of how to live and love honorably.

To my children, may you know how to live a life of honor before you are even old enough to read this book. Let this book be a reminder to you that things go well with you when you walk in obedience to God's Word and will. Mommy loves you.

Table of Contents

Foreword

The Honoring Life is a timely book needed for an honor less American culture. Honoring someone is no longer honorable. I was raised in the 60s when we gave honor to the American flag in the Pledge of Allegiance. We are now living in times where the pledge of allegiance is not mandatory in public schools.

This epidemic of lack of honor in American culture is prevalent with our children not honoring their parents (rebellion), married couples not honoring marriage (divorce), people not honoring civil law (crime), and the government not honoring life (abortion). Because of this lack of honor in American culture, we can see the collapse of the culture through the lack of respect for authority and growing anarchy.

The Honoring Life defines honor and why honor is important to you and your relationship with others. It's a book focused on women, honor and forgiveness, but everyone can learn from this book about living an honorable life.

The honoring of life begins first with honoring God. Once you learn why you honor God, honor for all others will become an honorable duty for you to uphold. Read it, meditate on the principles of honor and recall them, so you can obey them and see the results of living an Honoring Life.

Keith Graham
Pastor Now Word Covenant Church

Introduction

Before we get into the meat of the book, I thought it would be best if I introduced myself to you. My name is Tiffany, and I am a wife to my husband, Bryson, and a mother to three beautiful children. You might be wondering why I wrote this book and what makes me qualified to do so. I wondered the same thing. If you are reading this and you know me, you will know that I laughed while writing that last sentence. Initially, for almost four years, I wondered why the Lord would prompt me to write this book. *Why me*, I thought. Even after telling some that I would be writing it, I could see the "you're writing about honor?" look on their face as if to think I'm crazy to believe that God called *me* to do this. I was told this out loud as well. Regardless of what I or anyone else thinks, I'm the right person for the job. It took almost four years for me to decide to be obedient to completing this work. This is after I had every chapter outlined, all the research done regarding books written on honor and going back and forth asking God why. I mean, look at how much time I wasted. When I finally decided to write the book, I looked back at my proposal and realized, "Wow! I am qualified." Let me tell you why.

I'm writing this book from the perspective of someone who did not honor many people. I know what dishonor looks like. When you realize that you've already done something the wrong way and the Lord shows you the right way (whether through watching others, through rebuke/correction from those in a position of authority, or through the reading of his Word), you have a basis on which to share your personal experience and the truth that was revealed through it. I mean, isn't that where most nonfiction books come from? We share our life experiences, education, and what we learn from them all the time with those we encounter in one way or another. This is me doing just that.

I felt so inadequate, but God said otherwise. His word also says the same in 1 Corinthians 1:26-27: "For you see your calling, brethren, that not many wise according to the flesh, not many mighty, not many noble, are called. But God has chosen the foolish things of the world to put to shame the wise, and God has chosen the weak things of the world to put to shame the things which are mighty…." Me writing this has nothing to do with me and everything to do with what the Lord wants to say through me. He will receive all the glory from this because I need Him to complete this work. I pray that if there is something He is prompting you to do, you do it. Do it when you're afraid, or do it while feeling insecure or inadequate because He will get all the glory from your obedience. People will talk and doubt, but tune them out and walk out your purpose, for His glory.

I love to write, and I love this topic because it has brought so much healing to my life. When I got saved, I knew there was a lot that needed to change when it came to how I responded to authority. You can only use your personal life story as an excuse for so long. At some point, you have to acknowledge that you are responsible for how you respond to people. One major thing I learned about honor is that not everyone is an honorable person. However, if a dishonorable person is in a position of authority, you respect and honor that position. We will touch on that more in the chapter "Honoring Authority." I have not reached the end of my lesson on honor. I believe that just like any other area in our life, we continue to grow and be sanctified as we walk out our salvation. We should always be doing some form of work within ourselves to look more like Christ. I pray that this book will help you do just that. May the Lord renew your mind and prompt your heart as you read each page. May you walk in obedience to His word and will for your life, and may you find peace in knowing that no matter where you are, He loves you and is with you always.

Happy reading!

Tiffany Graham

CHAPTER 1

WHAT IS HONOR?

So, what do you know about honor? I've heard those words spoken to me before because the life I lived growing up didn't demonstrate honorable actions when it came to authority. I struggled with trusting those in positions of authority because of my personal experiences. Most of the people who had some level of authority over me had hurt me in some way. I saw people in leadership as waving red flags, and I didn't think they had my best interest at heart. I thought they were just going to hurt me the same way others had done before. When I played sports, I didn't respond well to the coaching methods used here in the United States (it sounded more like yelling to me). It's funny because when I think back to when I played sports as a child, prior to my parent's divorce, I don't remember having issues with my coaches. It's possible that my sensitivities to people shouting at me were heightened after the divorce. My memories of those years are cloudy. Anytime someone would yell at me, or tell me what to do, I would clam up and become triggered. Once that happened, I reacted with a fight-or-flight response. Usually, it was a fight. My sister said something to me that really gave me perspective regarding my level of disrespect toward people when I was younger. I'm thirty-seven now, so I'm referring to my childhood, teenage, and young adulthood stages in life. As we talked about my childhood, she recalled how bold I was. She said I always knew what I wanted and what I didn't, that I would express my boldness in a positive way through what I would wear or through singing out loud no matter who watched or heard. I remember being told that I would love to wear mismatched socks and didn't care what others thought. I still don't care too much, if I'm honest, about what others think about me. I spent a lot of time growing up guarding myself with others. When I was finally freed from that trauma, I decided I would always be my authentic self, whether people liked it or not and became pretty transparent as the years have gone by, owning my pain and triumphs. Obviously, there are boundaries and times where filters are required, but I chose not to become someone else for other people's benefit.

I am who I am unapologetically (there's a lot to unpack with just that statement), but I am authentically myself and work to be who God has created me to be.

I've had my struggles with insecurity in some areas, but I was predominately confident in what I felt or thought. When my spirit was broken, that boldness never left, it just turned into bold, defensive, disrespectful responses for self-preservation. I still expressed my thoughts, but now it was with more of an attitude or disobedience toward authority. It made sense that my personality never left me—it just shifted to a more defensive expression. Truly, I was just a scared little girl fighting on the inside not to be hurt again. I didn't know how to give people a chance to prove me wrong. It wasn't until adulthood where I realized that the people I didn't listen to growing up had high hopes for me and that their tone didn't always mean they were against me. I just needed to respond with honor. And this is not to say that people can't or shouldn't work on their tone when speaking truth to people. I believe you can speak truth in love without an aggressive tone. I say this because not everyone responds to things when they are said in a certain way. What I am saying is that regardless of how things are said, if there is *truth* in what is said, we should respond to that with honor and grace for the person delivering a difficult message. In hindsight, things could have been significantly different in my life. However, there is a reason the Lord allowed me to go through the things I experienced. He didn't cause the pain I endured, but He did allow it. He still protected me in the situations I couldn't, or didn't know how to, control. He also kept me safe from the irresponsible choices I made. Regardless of the decisions I made, the consequence that followed would be positive or negative. It was also my responsibility to respond to those consequences accordingly. I believe one of the reasons God allowed me to go through what I went through was so I could write this book in hopes that it will help others turn things around in their lives. So, let's get into it, shall we?

The Meaning of Honor

I hope it is safe to assume that you have heard the word "honor" before a time or two. I used to hear it occasionally growing up, but I don't remember being taught what it means, what it looks like, or what reward it comes with. I have found that people tend to merge honor with that of respect. I think you can have one without the other. According to *Oxford Languages*, "honor" means to offer high respect or great esteem to someone or something. It is "adherence to what is right or to a conventional standard of conduct." When you honor someone, you are able to see the value that person holds, and you respond to them with great esteem. Respect is having a deep admiration for someone, or something elicited by their abilities, qualities, or achievements. You regard their feelings, wishes, rights, or traditions according to *Oxford Languages*. What this means is that typically, honor is offered to people whom one respects. We admire them, so we respond to them with high regard, respect being the prerequisite. However, biblical teaching indicates that we should honor someone whether we respect them or not. No one taught me this, not formally anyway. It was just something I was supposed to know, and I came from a "do as I say, not as I do" type of environment. I can understand that philosophy, "respect them because they are your parents, or honor them because they are your parents, or teacher, principal, and so on." As an adult, I totally get it. But as a child, I had *no idea* what that meant. Now I will say this, I knew when I was being disrespectful because it felt wrong. Something in me knew when I was treating someone right or wrong. What I didn't know was the "why" behind it. I didn't understand what that word meant. I for sure didn't have the thought to go look it up or ask about it. Back then, you didn't ask questions, even when you had them. I believe that when the Lord speaks of honor, He wants us to treat people with high esteem and treat them in a way we would treat someone that we deem valuable to us personally. The reason why I believe this is so difficult to do is because there are people we should honor who don't necessarily do anything for us. The truth is we don't admire, let alone like, everyone. They haven't offered us anything or don't have any association with what is going on in our lives. The Lord wants us to honor people. Period. You have to determine what that looks like for you, and hopefully the rest of this book will help you on that journey.

Biblical Honor

So, what exactly does the Bible say about honor? Let's look at a verse that demonstrates *exactly* what honor looks like in the eyes of God.

> *Whenever the living creatures give glory and honor and thanks to Him who sits on the throne, who lives forever and ever, the twenty-four elders fall down before Him who sits on the throne and worship Him who lives forever and ever, and **cast their crowns before the throne, saying: You are worthy, O Lord, To receive glory and honor and power; for You created all things, and by your will they exist and were created.*
>
> (REVELATION 4:9–11 NKJV)

We should cast our crowns before the Lord and pass the crown to people. We should esteem them higher than ourselves (Philippians 2:3). Whoa! Let's let that sink in and marinate for a minute. Take a breath before moving on. That is some meat that needs to be chewed for a bit. Get all the flavor out of that verse! Ha ha…

Selah.

Ok moving on.

A common verse for honor would be Ephesians 6:2–3, which says, "Honor your father and mother, which is the first commandment with promise: that it may be well with you and you may live long on the earth." Why do you think Jesus said this? Why is this important for us to have learned as children? It clearly states this is the first commandment with a promise (notice I said with a promise. It's not the actual first commandment. That would be "Thou shalt have no other God before me." That means we honor who first? God.)

But I digress.

This verse shows the first thing Jesus tells children to do is to obey their parents. If this commandment is fulfilled, they will have a long life. I believe that being obedient as a child is a given. Things just work out better that way. But of course, as children, we think we know v a everything and want to do things our way. Ha ha. Most of us know this is just their way of finding out who they are and their personalities shining through. They don't realize the consequences of certain things or that there are negative habits that can be detrimental to them when they get older. Parents have lived longer and experienced things that children haven't. They know right from wrong (whether they practice doing right is a completely different topic), and they are called to train up a child so they will not depart from that training as they are older (Proverbs 22:6). But is simply being obedient showing your parents honor? I don't think so. I think that's where we start, but I believe the Lord wants us to take it further than just obeying. You can follow rules and orders without actually showing honor to someone. I call that submission to authority. A way that I have seen honor portrayed very blatantly is through service. My husband has a way of serving people that honors them. I didn't always think this was him honoring those people, especially his parents. I saw it as people pleasing. Boy was I wrong.

Ha, sidenote to any wives reading this: your husband is the head for a reason; and, if you have one that serves without regard to self, you have one that is modeling honor every day. Thank God for him!

Children can express honor to their parents by lifting them up in conversation to others, serving them by doing something they weren't asked to do, taking care of them when they are in old age, and so on. Imagine if this type of behavior started when you were a child. Despite what you may have gone through, if you understood what it meant and you wanted God's promise fulfilled in your life, what could life have looked like for you? This is why this book is so important. The more we know, if we make the choice to respond to the revelation of what honor is and why we do it, it could change the world. We could pour out this truth to our children and create a legacy of honor. It could change how people see one another. Instead of looking at a stranger with fear, we look at them with love and see the value they hold because they are a part of God's creation.

The Bible repeats this verse over and over because *honor* starts in the home. Everything we learn starts in the home, and it shapes how we respond to the world. I see this more and more as my children grow older. It takes a lot of energy to try to teach this principle, not to mention teaching everything else they need to know to become solid humans. It is a sacrifice that we, as parents, offer up unto the Lord to ensure we are training our children properly according to God's word. Taking the time to teach our children about honor honors God as well. He loves us, but He also loves our children and wants them to be able to be a light in this world. We honor God by modeling honor. Children don't learn by what you tell them, although most parents think this works. Children learn by what they see. You can tell a child not to do something all day, but if they see you do it, then they will eventually follow. They may also just do what you say, but when they get older, they realize you were all talk and no show, and they will run from what you attempted to teach them. Children have to see the firsts of your walk. They have to see us model good behavior, worship, prayer, repentance, forgiveness, and the fruits of the spirit. They can't learn from what they don't see. Did you honor your husband in front of them? Your wife? Were you disrespectful and manipulative? Do you dog each other out to other people or when your children are around? They see it all.

Now that you know what honor means and have a few general examples of what that looks like, think of some ways that you have honored people in your life.

Reflection

1. Have you ever been taught what honor is and what it looks like? If yes, what did you see growing up?
2. How can you honor the people in your life better today?
3. Take some time to think about what honor is and ask the Lord to reveal areas in your life where this can be improved.

*Use the journal space below to write down anything that came to mind as you were reading this chapter.

____

____

____

____

____

____

____

____

My grace is sufficient
for you,
for My strength is
made perfect in weakness...

2 Corinthians 12:9

CHAPTER 2

SIN

So now that you know what honor is and have a clearer depiction of it in your own life, let's get into the meat of things. What you're about to read is nothing short of uncomfortable and a miracle all in one fell swoop. You've probably heard about this before but more likely than not in the depth that you will hear—the topic of sin. Let's take a minute because a lot of people don't like that word. In the watered-down Christianity we have in the Western culture, sin is rarely spoken about after the gospel is given and received. We will get into that more a little later in this chapter. It's an uncomfortable word because it indicates that if we are in fact sinners, then we do need a savior, and for a lot of people, coming to that realization is extremely difficult. Think about when someone tells you about yourself. Let's say you have a friend who decides to be completely honest with you and tells you that you treat people horribly when you become scared of being hurt. Subconsciously, you hurt them before they can hurt you even though you don't want to lose their friendship. Hearing something like this, something very real, can be a blow to your whole day. In that moment you probably become very defensive and use explanations and excuses to justify that toxic behavior. This is what happens when people hear that they are sinners. Yet, it's still the truth. We are all born into a sin nature. Have you ever encountered a toddler who automatically knows how to lie and do it well? Ha! I have! I have three children. It's funny because sometimes I look at them and wonder, *Where in the world did you get that from because I know you didn't learn it here*. Sin can manifest in many different ways. It can manifest in bad character, fornication, stealing, dishonesty, and deceit (which is a sandwich of a little bit of truth and a lie). Basically, sin is anything that is immoral and does not glorify God—the one *true* God. According to the Bible, sin is a transgression of the law of God (1 John 3:4) and rebellion against God (Deuteronomy 9:7; Joshua 1:18).

> Sin began when Lucifer's pride got in the way and he wanted to be higher than God. Hence the saying "Pride comes before the fall." You can read more about this in Isaiah 14:12–15. Sin became an issue for the human race when disobedience from Eve manifested due to the deception of the devil in the Garden.

Jesus Christ came to earth and died for our sins, and the law was demolished, and we were made clean and holy in the eyes of God. Basically, God poured out His wrath on Jesus Christ and gave Him what we deserved, and He poured out His love for us. Jesus took our place and received God's wrath so that we would be made free and in the right relationship with Him for all eternity, as He originally intended. The prerequisite of this freedom, this forgiveness, is that we believe that Jesus came to earth, lived a sinless life and died for our sins on the cross. We also believe that He was resurrected after three days and was reunited with the Father in Heaven.

Selah.

Let's take a minute. If you know there is something missing in your life (maybe this is why you picked up this book) and you want to accept Jesus Christ into your life as your Lord and Savior, all you have to do, and it's very simple (not a fancy prayer), is acknowledge that you are a sinner in need of a savior. Tell the Lord you accept that Jesus died for your sins and washed your slate clean. He paid a price that no one could pay for you and invite Him into your heart. It's that simple. I will add this: if you don't know *anyone* that loves Jesus and follows Him (not just a Christian, but a follower), head over to my blog and send me a message, and I will try to help you find a church to get connected to. I know that is a large responsibility. However, if this book leads you to Christ, I feel an obligation to help you get connected to people who can help you. Although I would love to, I don't have the capacity to disciple every single person that may receive Christ, as their Lord and Savior, as a result of reading this book. It's not an easy walk, but it truly is the *most* rewarding and life-giving decision I have *EVER* made in my life.

> *For God so loved the world that He gave His only begotten Son, Jesus Christ, that whoever believes in Him should not perish but have everlasting life.*
>
> (JOHN 3:16)

One thing you have to realize about this life, this walk with God, is that it is you and Him. You need the church for fellowship and accountability; but you have to know God and the word for yourself. The closer you grow to God after making a decision for Christ, the deeper your relationship. It's like any other relationship in the sense that you have to cultivate it and invest in it for it to grow and flourish. Get to know the Lord through the Bible, and He will continue to reveal Himself to you more and more with each passing moment. You will grow in spiritual discernment and find understanding of things you never thought you could. The Holy Spirit who is there to help you on this journey will convict you. But listen, you're going to mess up. You're going to make mistakes and sin again, but the Holy Spirit is there to help you get back to where you need to be. Sin is a tricky thing. A lot of times, it feels good and fun. You get to live your life however you want and think that nothing is going wrong. The Bible says that the wages of sin is death. I believe that sin can lead you to physical death for sure. It can be fast depending on what you're into, or it can be a slow death. But this death is not just physical in nature. It is also a spiritual death. When the time comes for you to pass on, where are you headed? Think about all of the satanic and demonic references that are just blatantly out right now, especially in the entertainment industry. People say that Jesus wasn't real and that there is no God. If that were true, wouldn't that be true for Satan too? Can you have evil without good and good without evil? Why is Christianity the main religion attacked if there was no truth to it? Why are Christians targeted so much? It's because we know the truth. Our responsibility is to share that truth in love with those who don't know it.

> *Go therefore and make disciples of all the nations, baptizing them in the name of the Father and of the Son and of the Holy Spirit, teaching them to observe all things that I have commanded you; and lo, I am with you always, even to the end of the age' Amen.*
>
> (Matthew 28:19–20)

My prayer for you is that if you didn't already know Christ, you came to know Him after reading this chapter. I hope that whatever you are going through in this moment, you find comfort knowing that someone loved you so much that they gave up their own life so you could be free. That may sound absurd, but I have been through a lot of things that could have made me give up. Jesus rescued me in a time where I was tremendously broken in spirit and had no self-worth. There was no way I could honor anyone during that time, not just because I wasn't in that type of environment but more so because I didn't honor myself (I will talk more about self-honor in Chapter 7). Listen, if you haven't accepted Christ yet because you haven't gotten things "right" yet, or you have but you're waiting for some things to fall into place before you truly start following Him, just do it. Just follow.

God meets us where we are. There are a lot of people that will judge you when you start believing and following Christ. A lot of people have opinions that honestly don't matter. Don't allow yourself to miss out on the goodness and love God wants to share with you because people are judging you for your past or because you are your worst critic and feel unworthy. We are all unworthy and fall short of the glory of God (Romans 3:23). *Yet*, God still chose you! He wants that relationship and doesn't care what party you just left, drug you just took, or sin you just committed against others or yourself. He wants to know you. He wants you to know Him. Don't wait. I wasn't accepted when I came to Christ, not by most people. I felt judged, and I was criticized and chastised. It was one person who said some powerful words to me when I was about to give it all up and walk away because of the judgment. It changed the course of my walk, and it freed me in a way I didn't know was possible. I didn't strive to please people, but I decided to trust God and where He was leading me. And that decision led me straight into His presence like never before. My walk was a journey—is a journey. This isn't a sprint. It's a marathon, and most seasoned Christians forget to remember that and where they came from, so keep going. Believe. Accept. Choose today to tune out the noise and dial into the voice of the Lord. Please don't wait because there is so much that comes with your "yes." In the meantime, I hope you start learning more about the Lord and drawing nearer to Him during these difficult times. As He said in Matthew 28:20, "…I am with you always, even to the end of the age." He means it, and I can attest to it. Be encouraged and know that as we continue this honor journey, He is with us all, even me because I am still learning and growing like everyone else.

My Prayer for You

Father, in heaven. You are a good Father, sovereign and loving. You sent your only son, Jesus Christ, to earth to live a sinless life and die for our sins so that we can be able to have a relationship with You. I pray for those reading this book and ask that You meet them right where they are. Lord, comfort them in knowing that you paid the ultimate price so that we wouldn't have to. Speak to their hearts and draw them closer to You. Let Your Holy Spirit fall on them and guide them as they lay their old life down and begin their lives as new creations in Christ. You make all things new. You restore, revive, and renew all things. Thank You for watching over them and for Your promise to never leave nor forsake us. Thank You for Your grace, love, and mercy, and may they find joy in discovering how deep and wide Your love is for them.

In Jesus' Name,
Amen.

Change Your Mind

CHAPTER 3

WHERE DO I START?

Repent for the Kingdom of God is at hand.

(Matthew 4:17)

The first time I saw those words was on a billboard in Ghana while riding the bus to our next destination. It was summer of 2012, and I was on a mission trip with some church members. I remember looking at it and feeling scared and convicted. I thought about the urgency that jumped off that billboard. Those words stuck with me. They pierced my soul as I thought about what it would be like if the Lord came back during that time. Honestly, you hear the word "repent" quite often when you hear about sin. They go hand in hand. For me, I thought that repenting had a negative connotation to it. When you hear it in a message or teaching, it's coupled with a strong firm tone and can instill fear in you. It did for me until I realized what it truly meant. I learned about repentance during a women's prayer group that I was invited to. This group honestly changed my outlook on prayer and repentance. It even changed my outlook on confession, not the type of confession that you do in a Catholic church, in a box, with a priest next to you. No. I'm talking about true confession, a lifestyle of confessing your sins to God Himself and those who you are accountable to. Confessing your sins to people you trust allows them to walk with you as you overcome certain struggles or challenges life can bring. It brings forth accountability and provides you with a safe place to grow without shame or guilt. It frees you from the sin you are bound to and allows God to enter that space to provide healing, rebuke, comfort, and truth. I had that with some ladies in this group.

I remember the first time I attended; I was skeptical. I'm always on guard when entering a new space that claims the Lord is present. I believe it is important for us to guard our hearts and pray for discernment. Just because people say "God is present" doesn't mean He's there. Just because people teach the Bible doesn't mean it's taught properly or interpreted properly. Always pray for wisdom and discernment as you navigate new and old spaces. Stay in the word for yourself so you have the truth in you to recognize false prophets and wolves in sheep's clothing (Matthew 17). Build that relationship with the Lord so when things are off, you are able to recognize His voice in the midst.

I digress.

This first day of prayer was an experience I will never forget. I didn't say much, just observed. There were a couple of people I knew and most I didn't. Before prayer even started, we were preparing for communion. If you are familiar with communion, you know that our responsibility as Christ followers is to seek the Lord during praying, before taking the elements, to confess our sins and turn away from them (repent). Usually this is something you do privately with the Lord before the elements are presented because the majority of people do this at church. This is a practice we should have at home as well, and it was a practice that our prayer group had. The difference is that our host decided to confess her sin and repent out loud. As she did this, trusting the women before her (old and new), I was absolutely floored. I could not believe she said what she said out loud. It takes a lot of courage to confess your sin to those you are closest to, let alone do it in front of a group of women. But think about it. Isn't this what the Bible tells us to do? Now I am fully aware that not everyone needs to know your struggle or deepest secrets. A lot of people can't handle everything, and not everything is safe with everybody. Remember that. But at the same time, when you are with the body of Christ, we are to model Christ's behavior. We are called to love one another and carry each other's burdens (Galatians 6:2). We should have grace for each other's struggles and not forget where we came from and what we may be dealing with privately or in secret. We hold each other up and encourage one another. We are called to sharpen each other and edify our brothers and sisters in Christ.

Repentance frees us. My experience that day encouraged me to share my own sin and frustrations, and it created a lifestyle of repentance, openly confessing what I struggled with to my sisters who held me accountable while also encouraging me with their testimony. I became quick to repent and work on myself to become the woman God was calling me to be. Repentance doesn't lead us to condemnation but to forgiveness, freedom, and overcoming all that the enemy tries to use to keep us in bondage. God takes our sin and cleanses us. He then pours into us His truth and leads us to people who will walk with us through the struggle, regardless if it is minor or major.

So, what does it truly mean to repent? According to Strong's Exhaustive Concordance, repent in Greek is *metanoeo*, which means to change one's mind or purpose. It indicates spiritual conversion. It also leads to change after being with or to think differently after your decision to follow Christ. In Romans 12:2, Paul tells us, "And do not be conformed to this world, but be transformed by the renewing of your mind, that you may prove what is that good and acceptable and perfect will of God." This means that we make the choice to change our mind about our sin. We can choose to stay where we are and continue to live the way we do, with consequence, or we can change our mind and do the necessary work to persevere as we surrender to Christ. We choose. You choose, and I choose. I made that choice that day to do my best to repent swiftly and work diligently to change behaviors that I knew were not glorifying God.

It. Is. Hard.

But it is so worth it!

So where do *you* start? Take some time when you get a chance to ask the Holy Spirit areas that you have not confessed and released to God. As you sit in silence and think over some things that you may have not repented of or people you may have offended and/or even been offended by, write it down in the journal space and let the Holy Spirit guide you in the way the Lord wants you to address it. There is *no* shame and *no* condemnation. When you get to this place in your walk, the enemy will try to persuade you to think that your sin is too great for the cross, that you aren't good enough to be saved, or that the person you offended won't forgive. Don't listen to the lies. You are responsible for your response to your sin; that's it. Take the first step, and see what the Lord works out in you. Embrace the freedom that comes with confession and repentance. It literally changed my life. It honestly started my honor journey and has led me right here with you, reading this book. I smile knowing how much of a sense of humor the Lord has and how He uses those that not only feel unworthy but are least expected by the world to share such a message (i.e., me). Ha! *He can use anybody!* And if He can use me, *He most definitely* can use you! You are chosen, loved, wanted, and watched over. You have purpose, and I hope that your journey with Christ goes deeper as you encounter more of His grace as you continue to challenge yourself with the promptings in this book.

Sample Prayer

Father,

I thank you for Your kindness. I am grateful that You don't condemn me and shame me for my issues and struggles in life. Thank you for providing me with a safe space to share those struggles and my sin within them with You. I don't always know what to say or how to say it when I need to repent for something that has not brought You glory. I feel sometimes that I have to make things right before I come to You, but I know that is not true. It is a lie from the devil, and believing that lie can keep me from the freedom that You have so graciously died for on my behalf. Please forgive me for (insert sin). I thank you for Your forgiveness and ask that You help me overcome what I am struggling with. Mend my relationships, and give me the words to speak to myself and others to ensure that I am not falling back into what I have been acting out on. You are for me and not against me. Your word says that I can come to You with whatever I carry and that You will take my burdens and give me Your yoke, which is easy. I receive that today, Lord, and declare that I am made clean in Your sight through the blood of Jesus Christ.

In Jesus' Name,
Amen.

**I have to add this because I feel that it is necessary for whoever is reading this book and praying these sample prayers. The Holy Spirit hears you and affirms you and loves you and will walk with you *every* step of the way. I genuinely believe that your life will be changed as you challenge yourself to lay it down for His glory. After praying/writing this prayer, I sensed a great deal of the love that God has for you. My personal prayer is that your life will never be the same and you will encounter God in a way you have never before. May God bless you. – All love.

Repentance Journal Entry

CHAPTER 4

Forgiveness

Forgive and Forget

There is a phrase that I hear a lot when it comes to forgiveness: "forgive and forget." This is a phrase that I have used too many times, and it is one that is not necessarily realistic when it comes to the human experience. I usually hear these words come from the mouths of the people who need to receive forgiveness from someone. I know that I have said these words as a way to be forgiven and to not have to deal with the consequences of the offense I caused or the sin I committed. However, for those who were offended and victimized, they have a hard time forgetting what was done to them. Forgive and forget doesn't work for everybody. And when it comes to honoring people, depending on how you see forgiveness, the lack of forgetting may be what keeps you from giving honor to someone who has significantly hurt you.

We know that the Lord forgives and forgets. His word says in Ephesians 4:32 (NKJV),

And be kind to one another, tenderhearted,
forgiving one another,
even as God in Christ Forgave you.

Forgiveness, for some, can be instant. For others, it can be a lifelong process, a daily dying of oneself to lift up the heart of the Father over someone who we don't feel "deserves" the forgiveness they genuinely seek. Depending on the person and the offense, forgiveness can occur right away. Maybe the offense was minor, for example, stepping on someone's foot, or telling someone that you don't think their outfit looks right. You can assume that your honest words are helping them out yet could have completely killed off all confidence they had in themselves that day after getting dressed. As a woman, these types of comments can sometimes make or break a day, especially if you're hormonal or going through some things and just need encouragement. The initial response may be shock, and then anger, frustration, and worry about how to overcome the damage that was caused; but, once the apology is stated, the offense is done and both parties move forward. At least that's what we tell ourselves. Ha! Truthfully, sometimes moving forward after an offense means taking the negative thoughts captive until your confidence is built back up. I know I have been there. I have gotten dressed and felt very confident, and here comes Debbie Downer telling me I don't look good and should think about wearing something different. Like a ton of bricks falling from the sky, there goes my confidence. Have you ever been around someone that is just brutally honest and without tact because you asked their opinion? Yeah, I have a few of those in my life, and a lot of times it sucks, but I am so grateful for the people who are willing to tell me the truth about how I look and when my flesh decides to show up popping off at the mouth. These people have made me better. Period.

Let me get off of this tangent and back to the point.

Other offenses can be extremely heartbreaking and life changing. For me, this long-term, drawn-out offense, the one that impacted me the most, was that of my parent's divorce. This is an offense that not only broke my heart but also created new neural pathways in my mind that resulted in me putting up barriers and looking to control my environment as a way of not being hurt again. The behaviors that I developed, as I tried to prevent myself from being hurt again, only hurt me more. As I was trying to protect myself through controlling my environment, I lost control. Instead of allowing the Lord to do His work and heal me, I took my abandonment issues and victimized myself over and over again. One thing that God wants is for us to cast our burdens on Him (Psalm 55:22). We don't have the capacity to heal on our own; and although I believe in radical healing, I do not believe that this is a radical healing journey for the majority. Control, resentment, and my abandonment and rejection issues caused me to lose control and live a life of dishonor toward anyone that I felt could hurt me in any way. I dishonored my parents, my coaches, and any adult that tried to tell me what to do. I was a disrespectful brat, and it took me down a path that God never intended for me to travel. I had no idea what forgiveness was at the time and how true forgiveness would have completely released me from the bondage I was living in from all of that pain.

Holding on to Unforgiveness

A major setback for me was that I didn't know how to express my pain. I didn't believe I could talk to anyone about it or that they would understand. I held it in. Never hold in your pain. Think about what it would be like to hold blue flame in your hand. You will most definitely get burned. Our initial response would be to release that flame after the first burn because it hurts so bad. Now imagine touching the blue flame and deciding that instead of our reactionary, protective, response to move our hand away from it, we decided to hold on to it. What would happen? Our skin will suffer third-degree burns. Even further, the longer we hold on to the flame, the more we burn. Eventually our flesh will melt away, our muscles will begin to show, and so on. You get the picture. It's pretty graphic, isn't it? This is what happens when we hold on to unforgiveness. When we hold on to the pain of offense, our heart isn't just broken repeatedly, but it becomes hardened, dark. And our loving and honoring actions toward those we care about become bitter and mean.

God says in Matthew 18 that we should go to our brother when we have an ought against them. When there is an offense, we should call up our friends, parents, spouses, and even our children and tell them what we feel so that we can talk out the issue and reconcile with them. The excuse you hear a lot when people try to make it right with another is that "oh, they won't hear me out" or "they said they don't want anything to do with me." God says in Matthew 18:16, "But if he will not hear, take with you one or two more, that by the mouth of two or three witnesses every word may be established." So, He said go get so and so and bring them to try again—*try again*. He doesn't stop there though. He says in Matthew 18:17, "And if he refuses to hear them, tell it to the church." Do you see a pattern? The Lord is saying do not give up trying to reconcile. Relationships are important to God, and He wants to make sure that we have done everything in our power to salvage a relationship after an offense. I know for a fact people don't do this today. At least most don't. The church is the last step. If a person cannot forgive, if you cannot forgive, after the church gets involved, then you will be to one another like heathens and tax collectors (Matthew 18:17). Basically, He is saying you can move on and that you no longer have anything in common. But try, share your offense, and seek to forgive so that you can be reconciled. It is not until you are reconciled and have laid your pain at the feet of Jesus that you can honor the person who hurt you. Obviously, you can choose to just be kind and love people while talking behind their back, but is that true honor? True honor comes from within—from your spirit.

So, what about those offenses that occur frequently from the same person? I have a scripture for that too:

> *Then Peter came to Him and said, "Lord, how often shall my brother sin against me, and I forgive him? Up to*

> *seven times?" Jesus said to him, "I do not say to you, up to seven times, but up to seventy times seven. Therefore, the kingdom of heaven is like a certain king who wanted to settle accounts with his servants. And when he had begun to settle accounts, one was brought to him who owed him ten thousand talents. But as he was not able to pay, his master commanded that he be sold, with his wife and children, and all that he had, and that payment was made. The servant therefore fell down before him, saying. 'Master, have patience with me, and I will pay you all.' Then the master of that servant was moved with compassion, released him, and forgave him the debt...*
>
> (Matthew 18:21–27 NKJV)

There is more to this story. After the servant was freed from his debt, he went to collect a debt he was owed from another servant. He refused to show compassion; and when his old master found out, he ended up suffering the consequences that he had initially been freed from. Listen, the moral to this story is, forgive as many times as you have to. Period. Now, if there is someone taking advantage of you and the forgiveness you offer, use wisdom, and gracefully remove yourself from that relationship (if this is a marriage, that is a completely different topic with different ways to handle things. Seek godly counsel to assist you with forgiveness). If we do not forgive those who hurt us, God will not forgive us (Matthew 18:35). How can we expect to receive grace and mercy from the Lord if we are unwilling to extend such grace and mercy to others? Can you imagine how much hurt and heartache can be prevented if we walked out these principles in our lives? If we not only walked them out but also taught them to our children and modeled this lifestyle in front of them, our world would be filled with people who honor one another and choose to forgive and move forward.

I talked about forgiving and forgetting earlier in the chapter. What I believe God is saying about forgiveness is that we need to forgive people of the offense they caused us while not constantly reminding them that they offended us. If we are carrying an offense toward someone and they seek to make it right or we go to them to make it right and get free, constantly reminding them that they hurt us is not going to allow the relationship to reconcile and flourish. Dangling someone's sin over them just keeps them in bondage, whereas a lack of forgiveness for them keeps us in bondage. No one wins. To be honest, if you say you forgive someone yet constantly remind them of how and when they hurt you, is that truly the forgiveness God speaks of? God speaks of having compassion for the offender. He speaks of loving our neighbors (Mark 12:31) *and* our enemies (Luke 6:27). It isn't either or. Can you imagine loving and honoring someone *out of their pain*? Whoa! What a possibility of changing the world just by showing love, compassion, and honor to everyone we encounter in our lives.

Forgiving Yourself

Forgiveness is key to releasing the grip of the enemy over our lives and relationships. The Lord wants you to receive rest and wants you to release your burdens at the Throne of Grace. This includes forgiving yourself. Sometimes we can get so caught up in seeking out who we need to forgive that we forget to include our own transgressions. Forgiveness of self can eliminate the guilt we carry for the things we have done or for not forgiving others when we know we should. It can also tear down the walls that continue to build from fear and unforgiveness. Sometimes we have to forgive ourselves for not forgiving, and we have to release the shame that the enemy tries to put on us. The enemy will lie to you in a way that causes you to believe that you are not worthy of forgiveness whether by man or God, but we know that to be false based on His word and what Jesus did on the cross. That what you did or didn't do is unforgivable in the eyes of God, and you might as well just stay the way you are—stay silent. That is a lie from the pit of Hell, and you must know that you are worthy of God's forgiveness, as well as your own. You must know that Jesus died on the cross for you, for this very moment of time when you wake up and become aware that there is so much more covering under the Father when you choose to walk in forgiveness.

I want to give everyone the opportunity to receive healing on new levels as you continue reading. Follow the prompts to start this process, and may it turn out to be an opportunity for you to be free and reconcile relationships you have lost hope for.

Take a moment of quiet time (put on some worship music or anything that calms you in the space that you're in), and just listen for God's voice. Ask the Lord to lead you throughout this exercise.

1. Is there anyone that you need to forgive? Write it down.

2. Write out the offenses you have from that person or persons here:

____

____

____

____

____

3. Pray and release these offenses to the Lord, naming the individual(s) who hurt you and offer your forgiveness to them (sample prayer below). Is there anyone you are struggling to forgive? Write it down.

____

____

____

____

____

4. Talk to them to make things right (seek God's timing). If writing helps you form your words, use the space here.

Sample Prayer

Father, I thank you right now for Your sovereignty and grace for my life. I thank you, Lord, that You know exactly where I am and what I am going through internally and You still see me as Your daughter. You see me as Your beloved and pour out Your loving kindness on me. Your name is great, and I want to thank you for the cross, Lord. The very cross where You laid down Your life, I choose today to do the same. I choose to accept You and to walk in the freedom that You died for. I choose today to release anything that I have been holding onto that is not mine to hold. I thank you, Lord, now, for forgiving me for not releasing this to You when the offense first came upon me. I release (enter name of offender here) to You, God. I forgive them for the pain that they caused me when they (name offense here). I thank you that as I forgive them, You also forgive. I thank you that You are going before me now to restore the relationship and open the door for us to reconcile. I ask that You order my steps and allow me to be a light in the lives of those around me. Help me to show love, compassion, and honor to those who have not always had my best interest at heart and give me the capacity to show them how beautiful You are. May my prayers be solidified on earth as they are in heaven, and may I continue to pour myself out at Your feet as you Restore my heart.

In Jesus' Name,
Amen.

CHAPTER 5

HONORING GOD

In Chapter 1, I briefly touched on the difference between what the world considers honor and what God says about honor. In all things, before we offer honor to anyone else, all honor and glory should be given to the Lord. A beautiful depiction of what honoring the Lord looks like can be found in Revelation 4:8 NLT. This is where the twenty-four elders, or members of the heavenly Sanhedrin, sat along with four living beings. The four living beings repeated these words in verse 8 day and night, over and over again,

> *Holy, holy, holy is the Lord God, the Almighty—the one who always was, who is, and who is still to come.*

What is amazing in this verse, what stands out the most, is that they give God the glory and honor day in and day out. While this happens, the twenty-four elders pass their crowns to the Lord, laying them at His feet.

> *Whenever the living beings give glory and honor and thanks to the one sitting on the throne (the one who lives forever and ever), the twenty-four elders fall down and worship the one sitting on the throne (the one who lives forever and ever). And they lay their crowns before the throne and say, "You are worthy, O Lord our God, to receive glory and honor and power. For you created*

all things, and they exist because you created what you pleased."

(Revelation 4:9–11 NLT)

Wow! They lay their crowns at His feet. Can you imagine this? Day and night, night and day, waking up in the morning and laying all that you have at His feet. At the end of the day, all the praise and accolades laid upon you by your family and peers, you lay it down at His feet. You give it to God. It's His anyway, right? Anytime the Lord receives glory that we bestow upon Him, He, in the same step, receives honor from us. Would you do it? Could you do it? Are you doing it now? I'll be honest and tell you that although I give Him thanks as often as I can think of, I don't do this day and night. I don't think any of us do this day in and day out. We forget. We get comfortable, distracted, and haughty sometimes, and we forget to give God the glory that He is due. Everything we have is the Lord's. He allows it all because He is the Governor of our souls. He is our Creator, the Lord over all. Imagine what our lives would be like if we all put the focus on Him daily, moment by moment. Imagine how all worry melts away. Would there be time for anger, hate, envy, jealousy, and all the other negative things we encounter in our lives? If our focus is on the Lord, our sights would be set upon what is good and not evil. It's like what the scripture says in Philippians 4:8,

> *Finally, brethren, whatever things are true, whatever things are noble, whatever things are just, whatever things are pure, whatever things are lovely, whatever things are of good report, if there is any virtue and if there is anything praiseworthy-meditate on these things.*

There is a reason the Lord wants us to meditate on these things. He knows how life can get. But think about it. Isn't God all of these things? These things make up His character: things that are pure, true, noble, just, lovely, good, and virtuous. He is praiseworthy in *all things*! Amen!

So how can we practically honor God? What does that look like in everyday life? I would personally say that the first step in doing that is by walking in obedience to what He has instructed us to do. When we don't obey His word or do what we know is right, we are operating in sin. If it didn't register, disobedience is sin. Raise your hand if you've been disobedient. (I'm waving mine by the way cause boy have I not listened one too many times!) Whether it was out of fear, lack of desire, not wanting to die to self, and so on, we all do it. If you claim to be squeaky clean in this area, maybe take a minute and say a little prayer for the Lord to search your heart. Listen, we all have our moments, and we most definitely don't always walk in obedience when we should, but it's a great place to start. See everything flows from obedience. If we want all the Lord has for us, obedience is key.

> *But Samuel replied, "What is more pleasing to the Lord: your burnt offerings and sacrifices or your obedience to his voice? Listen! Obedience is better than sacrifice, and submission is better than offering the fat of rams."*
>
> (1 Samuel 15:22)

Samuel is speaking to Saul after the Lord commanded him to destroy the Amalekites. Samuel did destroy them; however, he kept the fatty livestock to sacrifice unto the Lord. He believed he followed God's command and thought he did even better by preparing. Sacrifice for him. Listen, sometimes God gives us instruction, and since we believe we know what God wants or we want to, in a sense, one up Him, we add to His instruction and try to do something we believe is pleasing to the Lord. God wants obedience. It's simple. If he says, "Take out the trash and put it in the middle of the driveway," that's what we should do. To us, putting it in the middle of the driveway doesn't make sense. So instead, we put it on the corner to make things more convenient for the garbage truck. This is not exact obedience, and yes, we will get it wrong (probably often), but we should do our best to carry out His commandments and instruction for our personal lives as He states. We don't need to understand the *why's* all the time. We just need to understand that He loves us and has ways and thoughts that are higher than our own (Isaiah 55:9). So, what happened to Samuel? Although his intentions were meant to honor and please God, because of his disobedience of not destroying everything, including the animals, he in turn rebelled against God. This rebellion and stubbornness (doing it halfway or his own way) caused God to reject him as king. This is why Samuel said that obedience is better than sacrifice. Remember this: intentions are great, but when our good intentions create offense or have a negative impact on someone or something in our lives, they cannot be used to justify our actions. We need to be accountable for the role we play in every situation, especially those regarding our response to the Lord's instruction.

Another way to honor the Lord is with your body. Now, a lot of us don't have a testimony of doing this very well, whether it is by marking it up with things that don't honor Him or by giving it away prematurely before marriage, and everything else in between. This includes the food we eat (guilty), what we drink (guilty), and not exercising to keep our bodies healthy (guilty again). Lawd (I know how I spelled it), I need some help in the area of food cause your girl loves a good meal. Ha ha! I love food, but my desire for the past few years has been to eat to live instead of live to eat, and I still struggle in this area. I feel as though I should be able to enjoy it because He gifted people with the ability to put certain foods and flavors together. I mean talking about it now, the whole context of this chapter could shift if I'm not careful. I'm kidding. Honestly, I believe sometimes that we struggle with caring for our bodies because in some way, we don't fully understand our worth and the amazing vessels

God gave us. We only get one. My challenge to you is to look at yourself and ask God what you can do or change to honor Him with your body. You better believe He will challenge you to do it. Also, disclaimer: be careful what you ask for.

Some other ways you can honor the Lord in a practical way are with your finances, seeking Him with your whole heart, and dying to self (we will touch on that more in the next chapter). Stewarding what the Lord has blessed you with, giving, tithing, and so on—these are ways you can honor Him with your finances (Proverbs 3:9). Tithing isn't the only way to do this. I know this is something you hear preached over and over in church, but there I don't believe that God will deny you if you don't tithe. I believe we tithe because we love God and we want to give Him the first of what He blessed us with, but He is not a God who just responds to how much you give to the church. He responds to the heart behind it—the trust He sees you have in Him. He's our Father. He gives like a father. If you have kids, think of what you give them. Do you only bless them when they do their chores and listen to what you say? I know we don't. Our kids are blessed and are given things because we love them. There is a context in which we teach that there are consequences for certain behaviors, but we don't deny them because they don't always listen. Our relationship is not conditional, and neither is yours with the Lord. We give because we love God, and because of our love for Him, we choose to be obedient to His word that instructs us to give Him a portion of our harvest.

> *Honor the Lord with your possessions (or wealth), and with the first fruits of all your increase; So your barns will be filled with plenty, and your vats will overflow with new wine.*
>
> (Proverbs 3:9 NKJV)

So, how do you choose to honor the Lord today? I encourage you to take some time to think about how you have honored God in the past and any areas that you may want to offer up to Him going forward. Below, you will find some scriptures you can meditate on and pray through. Ask the Lord to help you, to show you what areas in your life may bring dishonor to Him. And maybe there aren't any, and maybe there are some that show improvement. Just remember, you're doing this because you love God and you want to grow spiritually during this process. It's all about personal and spiritual growth, and the more we seek Christ, the more we find Him; the more we find Him, the more we get to know about Him; the more we get to know Him, the stronger our desire is to bestow honor unto His name; the more we give honor to God, the more we can honor the people He allows us to encounter in our lives. Imagine what that can do to our environment!

Happy meditating!

1. Purity (1 Corinthians 6:18–20)
2. Finances (Proverbs 3:9)
3. Living for Christ (Romans 14:8)
4. Seeking Christ wholeheartedly (Psalm 37:4; 1 Chronicles 16:11; Isaiah 55:6)

CHAPTER 6

Honor Thyself

Now, after honoring God, but before honoring anyone else, you must learn how to honor yourself.

Selah.

Let it marinate a little more.

Ok, if you meditated on that statement and your first thought was "Girl yes!" followed by a snapping of your fingers as if I just dropped some fire poetry that penetrated the core of your soul, you need to pause one more time and check your heart. Because honey, that ain't biblical. Yes, I said "ain't." If you can point me to a scripture that says we must honor ourselves, then cool. But before you do that, let me direct you to a few that say something completely different. Just sit tight with me while we unpack what I'm saying. Truly, I think there is a misconception about honoring yourself vs loving yourself and knowing your worth. The two are not synonymous.

Honoring Yourself

Let's start by saying this is a lie from the enemy and a theme for the culture. These days, everything is about the individual and what they can gain, how they can be accepted for who they believe they are, and esteeming themselves and their feelings above everything else. For believers, this is not a lie you want to believe. The Bible is very clear about how we should esteem ourselves. Let's take a look.

> *Let nothing be done through selfish ambition or conceit, but in lowliness of mind let each esteem others better than himself. Let each of you look out not only for his own interest, but also for the interests of others.*
>
> (Philippians 2:3–4)

Here Paul is talking about having unity through humility. Look at the phrase "lowliness of mind," which, in Greek, is *tapeinophrosyne*. *Tapeinophrosyne* means humiliation or humbleness of mind. It is a deep sense of one's littleness. It would be very difficult to honor yourself biblically if the Lord wants you to basically belittle yourself for others. Don't get caught up in thinking, *Oh, God wants me to diminish myself and be unworthy so others can feel worthy*. That's not what is being said here. It is an act of true humility, but Paul goes on to give an example of what that looks like. He is telling us that this type of mindset is the same mindset that Christ has. Although having the power to save Himself from the cross and "honoring Himself" over others first, He chose to humble Himself and take on the likeness of men. He relinquished His power to save Himself to the point of dying on the cross so He can be obedient to the Lord's will. Since he chose humility and laid His desire to live at the Father's feet, the Lord elevated Him and gave Him a name that would be above every other name (Philippians 2:5–11). This is why you can see that honoring yourself is not biblical, and it is important to understand the meaning of the words we use. To be honest, I wasn't initially going to have this chapter in the book. However, there were a few people I spoke to about the book who felt it was extremely important to be included. Even outside of the fact that my expressed goal was to help people understand what honor is and how we can honor God and other people in different roles in our lives, this point seemed to be pressing to share. So, I am sharing what I believe the Lord wants people to know. We are not to honor ourselves *first*. We esteem others higher. We look out for our interests, yes; but, we also look out for the interests of others, and we do it out of the pureness of heart, not to gain anything.

Imagine what our world would look like if we did this for one another. There are many things happening in the world right now where people are pushing their own agendas and beliefs on one another, almost trying to force others to be on their side so they can feel affirmed and approved of. What if we respected each other's differences (those saved and unsaved) and just loved one another? What if we chose to esteem those who are different from us higher than we do ourselves and looked to Christ for the internal affirmation we need? We could coexist not just with other believers who are different but also those who don't believe. We don't gain the world for Jesus by hitting people over the head with the Word. We win the world for Christ by sharing our own testimonies, loving how Christ loves, and speaking the truth in love to those in which we have influence. This all starts with relationships, first and foremost, with God and then others. It's pretty difficult to humble yourself and place someone else's needs above your own if you're not being filled, if there are significant voids in your life. This is why a relationship with Christ is so very important, not just believing He is the Messiah and that He lived and died for your sins but also choosing to get to know His character after you believe. There is *more* than just belief. There is so much more that the Lord wants to reveal to you about who He is, but just like any other relationship, the one with Christ has to also be cultivated. How do you do this? How is this even possible with someone you cannot see, touch, or hear? Let me tell you how I do it.

My journey with the Lord was not radical. There are some stories where people have had radical change. I didn't. I also knew that God was real and Jesus died for my sins. I thought I was a Christian. And, well, technically, I was according to the definition these days. Ha ha. But truthfully, I wasn't saved. I got saved on February 3, 2003. I walked up and received prayer and gave my life to Christ that day. And then everything was peachy! *Not!* No, it wasn't. I went back to college and just went back to my old life. I didn't read my Bible, didn't go to church, and just lived my life how I wanted. I went through a traumatic experience in college and moved back home and after being emotionally numb for almost a year (having literally no worth and believing I wasn't worthy of any kind of true love). I decided it wasn't the way I wanted to live. I know now that it was the Lord reminding me slowly of who I was and who I wasn't. I started my journey going back to church, serving in the ministry *while* being sanctified. Overtime, I gave God different areas of my life, and the journey was hard. There were a lot of things I had to acknowledge about myself, and I had to lay them at His feet, forgive others, forgive myself, and deal with consequences of my decisions. So much I had to do. It was hard, but the Lord brought people into my life that helped me walk it out. They were hard on me, telling me hard to hear truths about myself and what needed to be changed. But man, if they would have just told me what I wanted to hear and coddled me, I would not be anywhere near being whole at this time in my life. God doesn't promise happiness. He assures that there will be persecution and trials and things we go through that are hard (James 1:2–4). It only draws us closer to Him. He is made strong in us through our weakness (2 Corinthians 12:9). Humbling ourselves is hard, but there is glory in it because God is in it. You find your worth in Christ Jesus. You find your *worth* in Christ Jesus. *You find your worth in Christ Jesus!*

Please remember that! You are fearfully and wonderfully made (Psalms 139:14). The Lord knew everything about you before you were even born (Jeremiah 1:5). He has a plan for you (Jeremiah 29:11), and they are good. Even though we go through bad things and experience hard times, when you love and serve the Lord, please know there is always a greater purpose—always, and God uses what we go through to glorify and show others who He is. He is not a God that lies, He does not need anything from us. He wants a relationship with us. He loves us in the most beautiful way, and I believe that He wants to remind you, as you read, that this love is real and whole and true. It's for you, and as you receive it, you give it to others as well. There is no greater love than to lay your life down for your friends (John 15:13). In humility, we esteem others higher. Who are you going to do that for today? Who can you humble yourself before to show honor without complaint? If you don't know at the top of your head, take some time to think about it. It doesn't have to be someone you know. The world needs a little more of this attitude if we want to see any change happen.

Father,

I pray for the reader today. I thank you that they have made it this far in the book and pray that You have given them revelation through these words. I ask that You pierce their heart today. Bring them to a place of true repentance and recognition that they are in need of a savior. I ask that if they are already saved, You show them the areas that they have not given You yet. May they lay them at Your feet. May they humble themselves before You and receive the love You have so greatly poured out for them. Give them the strength they need to walk in the will You have for their lives. Give them peace knowing that You have a plan and all they need to do is surrender to it. I declare that fear has no place in their lives and that they take captive every intrusive thought that they are not worthy or enough. They are because you say they are. I declare your Word that You have not given us a spirit of fear, but a spirit of power, love, and sound mind. I acknowledge that You are always with us; therefore, we do not have to fear. I speak life over them right now and whatever they are going through, may You shine a light into those spaces, exposing the lie and reminding them of the truth of Your Word. I pray that they begin reading Your word and that they will not be overwhelmed by it. I pray they don't give up on it because of some lie or expectation that they have to be some bible scholar. May they start with one verse at a time and grow as You lead them. Reveal the truth of Your Word to them, and give them a desire to esteem others higher than themselves. May they know that their own worth and identity lies in You.

In Jesus' Name,
Amen.

CHAPTER 7

Honor Your Father and Mother

Where do I even begin? I want to share my testimony of honor and what it looked like for me growing up. First, let's start with a command of the Lord:

> *Children, obey your parents in the Lord, for this is right. "Honor your father and mother," which is the first command with promise: "that it may be well with you and you may live long on the earth."*
>
> (Ephesians 6:1–4)

Well, I can confidently say this was not my way growing up, especially with my mother. Not to make excuses, but there was a lot going on in our family growing up, and honor was nowhere to be found. My parents divorced when I was young, and it was extremely hard for me. My father made a promise to never leave, but he did (we have made amends in a significant way). Yet, it still crushed me. I was devastated and didn't know how to deal with those feelings. My mother suffered from depression and didn't have any capacity to lead our family in an emotionally present way. It felt as though I had to fend for myself most of the time. My brother dealt with the divorce in his own way, and that is his testimony to share, but I can say that we fought like cats and dogs. I know that this very long season of our life was trying for everyone. My mother was a believer and prayed for our family constantly, but this wasn't a topic that was taught, nor was it something that I was shown through action growing up.

I knew that I was disrespectful and rebellious, just really acting out in a negative way because I needed attention and love, but I didn't know that it was a lack of honor toward my mother that I showed. I didn't even know what it meant back then, nor had I heard it discussed growing up. I was familiar with the scripture, but being discipled at a young age and having someone explain the concept was not what happened. It's funny because things are expected of children, yet adults fail to understand that behaviors in children are learned. We watch and we do. I know this now more than ever because I have three of my own. Anyway, not to get into my full testimony because that is a book within itself, I didn't honor my parents, and my father wasn't honored from a distance. I respected him and honored him while in his presence, but over the years of growing up and with him not being active in our life, I grew cold toward him. There are some very specific reasons for the chill he received from me, but it's not necessary to address. I am happy and blessed to say that after many talks with my parents, apologies, and seeking forgiveness and repentance to the Lord, I do my best to honor them now. Sometimes we don't get it right. Everyone's story is different. What matters is that when you are made aware, you make the change. You make things right. No excuses, make the choice. That is what I did. My husband had a lot to do with this change in my life. I used to think that he just did whatever his parents said and didn't have a mind of his own (I was allowed to pretty much do what I wanted with no discipline), but I know now he honored his parents, truly, in the way God designed us to. He has a mind, he has a choice, and they have never forced him to make any decisions he didn't want to outside of what their basic rules of the home were. He had to respond with obedience to their rules and instruction. As an adult, he still honors them and seeks out their guidance. It's funny because we were just talking about seeking out wisdom from our elders to ensure we don't go down the wrong path. I believe this is why my husband has been so blessed. I mean, he oozes favor from his pores. This is not to say that he hasn't had trials and difficulty in life, but overall, he is tremendously blessed.

God's word says that if children honor their parents, things will go well with them. Let me tell you. I've had a lot of favors in my life. However, I have also had a lot of heartaches. When I look at my life and think about the decisions I made and how my mother would give me certain instructions that I didn't follow, pain and disappointment usually met me with a sweet kiss. I didn't respect my mom, for many reasons that I now understand as an adult. I was also angry with her. I say anger, but truly it was just hurt. I was hurt that our life was turned upside down and that I didn't understand what was happening. I also blamed her and wanted her attention. She was all I had. For most of my upbringing, I felt alone, and because of that loneliness, I sought out attention in the wrong spaces.

Honoring people, especially our parents, is a choice, just like anything else. We choose to give honor just as much as we choose to love. And giving honor to our parents even when we are hurting or frustrated with them builds our character and teaches us to honor others outside of our home. It is a learned behavior, and it should be taught to children and not just expected from them. Children who see honor walked out in their own home will learn how to implement it. I think we should also go further to explain to our children what it means and why we do it. The rewards come, and we don't just honor so we can attain something from the Lord; that would be seeking to honor for self-ambition and promotion. No, we choose to honor our parents and others because we love the Lord and His Word.

There are a lot of homes without a father. If you look at how children act out now, you will almost always find that there is no father in the home. They carry authority and presence. The nuclear family is dwindling, and it's so unfortunate. But there are many father figures, and I pray for those homes who don't have a father present for whatever reason. I pray that the Lord will bring godly men into the lives of children who lack in this area.

I was rebellious, which is a common characteristic of children who don't have both parents in the home (mostly, this isn't true for every child or home). Keep in mind that no one in my home was emotionally healthy at that time. We were all dealing with grief, loss, and some level of depression. I was looking for love and attention in all of the wrong ways and had no idea. I made terrible choices with how I treated my mother, and it was just mean. Hurt people hurt people, right? Yes, that's true, but we can change that one family at a time. I think what is important is that wherever we are in life, we honor others (especially our parents) so that we can be a witness of honor to whoever we are around.

Children, honor your father and your mother no matter what you think about them. You don't always know what they are going through, and you are responsible for yourself. Obviously, I'm speaking to every adult who is a child. But, if you have children of your own and this isn't a topic that you are exposing to them, start now. You will not regret it.

Things to ponder:

1. Did you grow up knowing what honoring your father and mother looked like?

2. Did you honor your parents (whether they were together or not)? How?

____

____

____

____

____

____

3. If you didn't honor them growing up, how can you walk out an honoring life toward them now (if they are still with us)?

____

____

____

____

____

4. If you didn't honor your parents well (for whatever reason) and they are no longer living, know that the Lord is still with you and there is no condemnation. Use the space below to write down whatever it is you would tell your parents if they were still alive and find healing and grace at the feet of the Father.

CHAPTER 8

HONORING AUTHORITY

Greatness
Is
Serving

Authority. You can look around the world today and see that there is a significant issue with people honoring authority. One of the main reasons, I believe, is because those who walk in authority take advantage of it and therefore abuse the power that they hold. Whether they are biblical leaders, law enforcement officers, politicians, teachers, or executive overseers, people in authority have a history of starting off with the right intentions and falling down the rabbit hole that they are more important or significant than those who they lead. We know this is not true and that this is most definitely not the way the Lord leads. There is a lot to unpack when it comes to honoring authority, so let's start with the blueprint, shall we?

The Blueprint for Leadership

When Jesus came to reveal Himself as the Messiah, people expected Him to come in an extravagant way. They wanted to receive their King, and according to them, He should have rode in majestically. That's what kings do right? Not this King. He came in on a donkey. Imagine hearing that the President of the United States was expected to come, and when he finally does, instead of showing up with tons of security, a long line of cars following behind, and a nice suit, he shows up in a Prius wearing jeans and a Walmart T-shirt. Thinking of it, it's kind of funny, don't you think? Could you imagine that? Your response would be, "What in the world is wrong with him? He can't lead looking like that!" Well, this is probably what everyone thought when Jesus arrived. For those who had higher expectations, they were definitely disappointed. However, this entrance was intentional, as is everything that the Lord does. He was sending a message. The first message was, I think, that how people look or arrive does not determine their purpose or power. But more importantly, He came lowly—humbly. It makes sense because He came from heaven to earth, and He came to serve and not be served. Check out the following:

> *You know that the rulers of the Gentiles lord it over them, and those who are great exercise authority over them. Yet it shall not be so among you; but whoever desires to become great among you, let him be your servant. And whoever desires to be first among you, let him be your slave—just as the Son of Man did not come to be served, but to serve, and to give his life a ransom for many.*
>
> (Matthew 20:25–28 NKJV)

Let's look at the Message version:

> *Jesus, knowing their thoughts, called them to his side and said, "Kings and those with great authority in this world rule oppressively over their subjects, like tyrants. But this is not your calling. You will lead by a completely different model. The greatest one among you will live as the one who is called to serve others, because the greatest honor and authority is reserved for the one with*

> *the heart of a servant. For even the Son of Man did not come expecting to be served but to serve and give his life in exchange for the salvation of many."*

BOOM! Right there is your model! I love this so much. Can you imagine our leaders actually serving to benefit those they lead instead of the other way around? If we all led this way, it could change everything! So here is your foundation. You may be wondering if you should still honor those who are dishonorable or who lead like tyrants. The answer is yes. A resounding *YES*! How you treat people and honor them says more about you than them. Maybe some people deserve mistreatment because of how they treat others. That's not for you to decide even though it is hard. It's not our responsibility to make them pay for how they treat others. If you honor them, even when they don't deserve it, the Lord can use that and intervene, especially if you add prayer to that.

It is hard! Y'all, we are naturally emotional beings, but we should not be led by our emotions (Jeremiah 17:9). When has responding out of emotion ever really worked out for you? True strength is found in operating out of self-control and wisdom, and we have to seek that out from the Father. People don't win just because they are compliant or submissive to authority. Christ wins, and, in turn, you win! So be encouraged and know that God will use your obedience to honoring those in authority to shine

His light where there is darkness. And remember, you're honoring the person in authority because of who they are or even their title necessarily. You are honoring them because you know that God allowed them to be in that position, for whatever reason, whether they are there to grow or because the Lord is allowing you to grow through encountering them. He appoints *all* leaders.

> *Daniel answered and said: "Blessed be the name of God forever and ever, For wisdom and might are His. And He changes the times and the seasons; He removes kings and raises up kings; He gives wisdom to the wise and knowledge to those who have understanding. He reveals deep and secret things; He knows what is in the darkness, and light dwells with Him."*
>
> (Daniel 2:20–22 NKJV)

Romans 13:1–5 says, "Let every soul be subject to the governing authorities. For there is no authority except from God, and the authorities that exist are appointed by God. Therefore whoever resists the authority resists the ordinance of God, and those who resist will bring judgment on themselves. For rulers are not a terror to good works, but to evil. Do you want to be unafraid of the authority? Do what is good, and you will have praise from the same. For he is God's minister to you for good. But if you do evil, be afraid; for he does not bear the sword in vain; for he is God's minister, an avenger to execute wrath on him who practices evil. Therefore, you must be subject, not only because of wrath but also for conscience' sake."

Whew! When you resist authority, you are resisting God's divine order because He appointed that authority! Lord have mercy! I wish I would have known and had the revelation of this growing up. When you think of this scripture and look at what is going on in the world, are you surprised? He tells us very clearly that if we do good by honoring those in authority and just generally in our lives, we will not have to fear authority. Oh, how I love His Word and the encouragement it brings. We don't have to respond to fear mongering with fear. We just simply, very simply, need to be obedient to the Lord and submit to those He has placed in positions of authority, and things will go well with us. No fear. Fear is a liar anyway.

I think of how many incidents have occurred with the police in the past few years and how a lot of issues have resulted in death or citizens getting hurt. A lot of people do not respect the police because there are many who are corrupt. There are many that aren't as well. Regardless of who you encounter, our responsibility is to submit to their authority even if we are wrongfully targeted. We are called to submit. If they pull you over, submit, and respond to their requests compliantly, even if they may be wrong. The same thing goes for other leaders. And listen, if you have a specific or isolated situation, seek counsel. I'm simply pointing out that God has called us to honor those in positions of authority because He placed them there. He will deal with their abuse of power or wrongdoing. And let's not just harp on those who do wrong; this is for those who are amazing leaders too. It's easy to submit to a good leader though, right?

I recommend you read all of Romans 13. And read it in different translations; read a commentary. It's simple and encouraging because if you love the Lord and want to walk in His ways, this is one very significant way to do it. You will always have some kind of authority over you.

I didn't honor all authority. I struggled with honoring my mother, coaches, or anyone who could have been an authoritative figure because of fear and hurt. I didn't respond to tough love or aggressive instruction. I still have a hard time with it sometimes. Although now I look at people's character and intention and since I have a closer relationship with the Lord, I can respond in submission or respect to someone in authority. It doesn't mean you won't disagree or have conflict, but you can honor and respect those in authority with how you handle the conflict you're in. We are all growing, and my main focus at this time in my life is to try to teach my children the importance of honor. I intend to share my experience with them and how difficult things were for me growing up while also allowing them to see my husband's experience and how things went well for him. We are a blueprint for them. They have two parents who had experiences on both sides, and I think they are blessed to have that because they will be able to see the fruit that was produced from both sides.

Where are you on this journey? Do you struggle to honor authority in general, or do you just struggle to submit to people who abuse the authority they have? Regardless of which one it is, remember that the Lord appointed them; and your responsibility is to do good, honor them, and let the Lord handle the rest.

Write down your experience with authority.

Why do you think you respond to authority the way you do?

____

____

____

____

____

____

____

How can you change how you respond to authority?

____

____

____

____

____

____

____

> Therefore, submit yourselves to every ordinance of man for the Lord's sake, whether to the king as supreme, or to governors, as to those who are sent by Him for the punishment of evaders and for the praise of those who do good. For this is the will of God, that by doing good you may put to silence the ignorance of foolish men—as free, yet not using liberty as a cloak for vice, but as bondservants of God. Honor ALL people. Love the brotherhood. Fear God. Honor the king.
>
> (1 Peter 2:13–17)

Meditate on the foregoing scripture. What do you think the Lord is revealing to you?

____

____

____

____

____

____

____

When you finish, continue reading the chapter. It's good, convicting, and will, for certain, change your view on how you should respond to those in leadership moving forward.

Remember, vengeance is the Lord's, and honor is our response to God's will and goodness.

CHAPTER 9

An Honoring Marriage

I just have to say that this is a tough topic, especially when you have expectations or standards you want to live by in your marriage. Keep an open mind. Just because I am writing about this doesn't mean I always get it right. I feel that is important to say. We can know what to do, but it is important to do our best with implementing what we know. I believe that hard work on ourselves pays off, and I've done a lot. I haven't arrived and won't until I'm made complete when the Lord returns. Until then, the Lord will continue to sanctify me for as long as I surrender myself to Him. This means, for as long as I open up to the truth of who I am and how I think, act, and respond to every situation in my life. Transparency is *key*. It is vital if you ever truly want to grow. It takes maturity to look inwardly and acknowledge things that need to change. Come on this journey with me. The Lord is the only one watching at this point, and He already knows who you are and what you're thinking anyway. It's not like you can hide from Him, even though we all try sometimes. Be brave as we talk about honor in our marriage. As you read, do your best to think about yourself and how you can improve, as opposed to what your spouse needs to change to make you "happier."

So, who is ready to dig deep into an honorable marriage? I'm speaking mainly to the ladies here because it is not my place to instruct a man. However, if you are a man reading this, I recommend seeking the Word and counsel from another (godly) man if this is something you struggle with. There may be some things here that you can apply to your life, but I'm writing from experience and what the Word says for women in marriage.

Ladies, there may be some things I say that challenge you and cause conviction. Trust me, I've already been there and walked through it. And guess what? I'm not done walking it out. I will never be done because this is a daily choice and there are days where I get it completely wrong, even with knowing what I should do.

Wives, honor your husband. What does that look like? Let's look at what the Lord says. In Hebrews 13:4, it says,

> *Marriage is honorable among all, and the bed undefiled; but fornicators and adulterers God will judge.*

Let's take heed that honor in marriage is between both the husband and wife. However, the Lord specifically instructs men to honor their wives (1 Peter 3:7), and for wives to submit to their husbands as unto Christ (Ephesians 5:22). I didn't find a specific scripture that outlines the instruction to "honor" the husband, but we don't need one that specifically says that. It doesn't need to include that word for us to know it's a command of the Lord. That is because we are instructed to submit to our husbands as unto the Lord. If we are acknowledging our husbands and reverencing them as we do Christ, honor is included in that, not to mention that the Lord instructs us to honor everyone, so wouldn't that include our spouses?

Sometimes honoring our husbands when we see the whole of them is difficult. No matter what we encounter in marriage, it is our responsibility to set the tone and stage of what honor looks like, especially if we want our children to learn how to honor their spouses/marriages as well as other people. Everything starts in the home.

I can tell you that this was not easy for me. I thought it would have been, but as the Lord sanctifies us in marriage, we encounter different layers of one another that may not be so appealing. It takes self-control and choice to honor someone you love who may have said or done something hurtful to you. Regardless of what the popular belief is, we can honor our spouse even in the toughest of times if we choose to. (Keep in mind, I'm not referring to anyone who is being put through abuse. If that is happening, please seek help and guidance from someone to get out of that situation.)

I found it difficult to honor my husband when he has hurt me or when we are just going through some growing pains. However, when I started doing things the Lord's way and shut my mouth and stopped trying to control my environment, things changed. I changed. He changed. God changed our environment.

I encountered some bad relationships and had a lot of hurt and fear that was still lingering. I didn't realize this until the commitment was made, but one thing that changed me was my choice to find healing, no matter how hard it was. And believe me, it was hard. As you heal, things come out, resentment and bitterness can form, and so on. I'm not saying this was prevalent in our marriage, but we walked through some healing together. I was being poured out in front of him; and he got all of my fear, however it manifested on a particular day. In turn, it seemed as though he built up resentment and frustration towards me. It was hard. It was also necessary for us to be fused together on our journey to become one in the flesh. If you believe that marriage is easy and doesn't come with challenges, you are sadly mistaken. It's not easy, but not being easy doesn't mean it has to be bad. I saw how marriage was treated between my parents, and I learned some behaviors that were not healthy that I took into my marriage without even realizing. When my husband would call them out, I thought he was just trying to be hurtful. What I love about our journey is that the Lord slowly opened my eyes to behaviors and thought patterns that my husband would point out, and as I began to grow out of those habits, my husband showed grace and love. I'm pretty sure there was also a sigh of relief from him on some occasions. Ha! Like, "Finally! Yes!" I laugh as I think about it. What I love about it is that he stepped back and just let God finally take control and vice versa. You are not your husband's Holy Spirit and he isn't yours. In everything, we have to go to the Lord with prayer and seek wisdom. We cannot change our spouses. We can only be responsible for ourselves. It's hard, but if you just get out of the way, the Lord can work a lot faster. Complaining also doesn't work. So how did I come to honor my husband? Well, I did and continue to do my best not to argue. I also just simply express my needs, and if there is something that is lacking, I take it to the Lord. I don't seek to be happy, nor do I seek out my husband to make me happy. Only the Lord can bring me true joy. But if he is having a bad day or I'm reading too deep into how he is responding, I just have to let it go and take his word for it. I had to let go of how I thought he should discipline or parent our children. If I was triggered by something he did, that's on me. His intentions are pure, and he loves our family very deeply. You have to recognize your own triggers and work through them. I started talking to him about different things and making recommendations, and we found common ground. That only comes when you respect your spouse. You have to know who they are and what their character is and what their intentions are. Test those intrusive thoughts and assumptions. Ask questions. Have conversations. Communication is so important. *Accept* who they are, and when it comes to who they are not, pray. Serve them as Christ came to serve. Fulfill your role in your marriage that you are responsible for. If you don't have set roles, talk about it so that when you are being held accountable, you don't get all snippy about them holding you accountable. I struggled with the word "roles" for a long time. Like, "Who are you to tell me what role I play," blah blah blah. I mean, I was a janky mess because I wanted him to communicate with me in a certain way. Listen, yes there are ways things can be said respectfully, but again, check the heart. And trust me, things will get better, and both parties are more willing to bend and change for the betterment of the marriage when honor and respect are evident.

What was it like growing up in your household? How did you parents talk to one another? Are they still married? If not, think about how that shaped your view of marriage or even the fear of whether or not yours will last in spite of you wanting it to? Do you live in fear of rejection and abandonment? Are you afraid to lose yourself if you decide to serve and honor your spouse? Do you feel like you're losing in some kind of way because you are the one who apologizes or forgives first every time? Let me tell you, you're not losing the game. It's not a game. It's not a race. The way you serve according to God's word may honor your spouse, but ultimately it honors God. If you cannot bring yourself to serve your spouse and family the way the Lord wants you to because your marriage is currently strained, then be reminded that you are honoring the *marriage* and walking in obedience to Christ. So, if you have that "I'm not letting him win" mentality, realize that you're also responding to Christ this way.

So how have I honored my husband? Well, I try my best to keep the home in order. I am not always able to clean the whole house on weeks we don't have the cleaners come because we have three young ones and there's just so much to do in a day. But I try to keep the living space, bedroom, and kitchen in order before he gets home. I do my best to have dinner ready, and if it's a day I don't feel like it or can't get to it in time, I make sure we get dinner somewhere (which has been often in this past year or two, ha ha). I also have worked on not leading the charge in parenting or correcting his parenting style (which is different from mine). We have the same end goal for parenting our children, but we are different when it comes to delivery in some cases. We make each other better, and we learn from one another. The most important thing is that we are sending the same message to our kids and that they know we are unified. Do we always get this right? Absolutely not! We are not perfect, far from it. But we do our best, and we are accountable. He appreciates when my car is clean, so I've recently implemented making a point to vacuum and declutter it when I get a chance. Typically, it's filled with toys and clothes because we spend a lot of time in it. I'm trying to focus on things that don't cause him more stress, and as I have done these things, he loves me in the ways that I need. He typically does that anyway. He recognizes that staying at home is hard and taxing, but just as I sacrifice, he sacrifices big time too. Very big! And we are so grateful to him for it. The way we honor one another can change over time too because seasons change.

Right now, we are in the thick of having young children. Dealing with all the emotions and challenges that come with this season of life, we make a point to make time for one another which is extremely important. Again, we don't always get it right. We struggle and it's hard, but we allow the Lord to lead, and we do our best to communicate with one another. Where we miss the mark, the Lord fills in the rest. Keep at it and know that it is extremely important to look inwardly. Ask the Lord to check your heart, and when He checks you, respond obediently. The Lord knows our spouses better than we do, and He knows how to lead us. We just have to decide whether or not we are willing to follow Christ fully in our marriage, trust Him fully, and die to self. Daily death. Daily. Death. I know, I know, that's hard. But do it because Christ did it for us and gave us the blueprint. Take the picture of your spouse out of your mind and recognize that everything we do is unto the Lord. The same goes with not fulfilling his will or walking in disobedience. If you are not doing what the Lord told you, you do that to Him, not your spouse. Not a good place to be. There is no peace there, no joy. Try God's way before you do anything that may jeopardize what you could have in your marriage. It's a moment-by-moment choice. And it is not easy. But it is so worth it.

I took an anonymous survey regarding honor in marriage. There were five questions I asked:

1. Define “honor”.
2. What does honor mean to you in your marriage?
3. How do you honor your spouse?
4. What does your spouse do to make you feel honored?
5. Do you think you can do better in this area? If so, how?

I love the answers, some detailed and others straight to the point. I wish I knew who answered what now because I would dive a little deeper on some of the responses given, but overall, I think the consensus of what honor is was the same across the board. For some, it’s possible they just answered as they thought they should, and for others, I could tell there was more thought put into the question based on how they answered and the transparency of their answers. As you ponder these questions for yourself (if you are married), the main thing I want you to know is that *no one* has arrived. We may know what honor is and how to implement it in different areas of our lives, especially marriage, but it doesn’t mean we get it right every time. What I adored about some answers are that people know their spouse and what they need, but when they got to the last question, they were honest that they don’t always get it right and that they could improve in certain areas.

A common theme was husbands loving their wives and wives respecting/submitting to their husbands (Ephesians 5). Some equated honor to celebrating their spouse as who God made them and upholding vows. I found answers that spoke of selflessness, transparency, and "stepping outside of themselves to lift the other up without expectation of anything in return" (I really like that one; this can be hard to do especially if you feel that your needs aren't being met). People spoke of being adored by their spouse who loves them with their personal love language. A lot of times we can love others in the way that we want to receive love. It's easier because our personal love language is a natural way for us to show others love since that's how we love ourselves. It's a lot more challenging to love someone in the way they receive love when it looks different from how we like to receive love. It requires self-sacrifice, patience, effort, time, and grace. If we are running on empty, it's even harder, and yet, this is what we should be doing if we are choosing a life of honor. This is what Christ did. He put Himself and His desires aside for our own and for the will of the Father. He had the ultimate self-control because He also had the power to rescue Himself, and yet He moved toward the cross, toward the danger, for the bigger reward—our souls. He is the blueprint of how we should love our spouses. Husbands, love your wives as Christ loves the church, and wives, submit to your husband. Another scripture says the following:

> *Husbands, love your wives and do not be bitter toward them.*
>
> (Colossians 3:19 NKJV)

Why do you think Paul wrote that? Is it possible it was said because us women can make things difficult sometimes? We can lack respect and honor and cause our husband to become bitter? Maybe. I'm pretty sure that's very possible, even likely. Is it also possible that it was written because husbands have to actively forgive and lay down their lives for their wives (as Christ did for the church), and if they are not actively doing this, a bitter root forms in their hearts? Ways of improvement in this area are to have clear communication and to actively listen to your spouse and their needs. Truly listen, engage, and give undivided attention when they are expressing their needs, even if they seem remedial or insignificant to you. Your spouse's needs are important, and sometimes, truly, they just want to know you hear their concerns, and try to empathize with them (understand them by relating to their feelings in some way or another). Remember that your spouse is a reflection of who *you* are. If you see things in them or call things out in them, it's important to check your heart first and seek the Lord to search it so He can reveal anything that needs to be worked on. I do my best to work on the areas that the Lord reveals to me. It is *hard* work. It's draining, I mess up; but I want to look more like Christ, so I do the work. There has never been a time that it wasn't worth it. If you are not intrinsic enough to look at yourself first before pointing things out in your spouse, it is possible you deal with pride and lack the accountability needed to address areas in your life and character that need pruning. I encourage you to get rid of the dead areas so the Lord can breathe life back into those dark spaces. When I say dark, I mean dark because we know that whatever is in us that is not like Christ, it must come from our flesh. We want to walk in the Spirit, and I can tell you now that when I'm not tuning into the Holy Spirit, the fruits of the Spirit lack in my life. I cannot operate in His fruit without Him. That's why they are called the "Fruit of the Spirit" and not the "Fruit of Tiffany". Put your name in there 'cause you don't have His fruit without Him either, okay. We cannot live a life of honor in our own strength. We just can't.

When you get a chance, after answering those questions, take a look at your spouse and thank God for them. Change just one thing that you could do better to honor them today, and focus on yourself, serving without expectation of anything in return, and trust God as you wait to see the change in them. Remember, you can only be responsible for yourself and how you serve them and others. God will take care of the rest.

CHAPTER 10

AN HONOR INHERITANCE

As you reflect on everything you have read so far, I want to encourage you that as you honor everyone, regardless of the place they hold in your life, you are walking in obedience to God's word. Remember that everyone should be honored according to the Word of God, simply because He said so and because everyone was created in His image. Now, realize that we are all created in His image, but not everyone has made the choice to follow Jesus. You can be the vessel He uses to do this as you share your testimony (Matthew 5:16; Revelation 12:11) and honor those as Christ would. We choose to honor others because we choose to honor God and be obedient to His word. The consequence of that choice (not the why) is the blessing that comes from honoring others.

Things Will Go Well

He promises us that if we honor our father and mother, things will go well with us. We address this in the chapter about honoring your father and mother. I can attest that as I did not honor my parents growing up, things were difficult for me. Because I didn't listen to instructions regarding certain areas of my life, I found myself alone, mistreated, abused, and put in situations I really didn't want to be in. Was this God's fault? No, it was mine because if I had listened, I could have avoided about 90% of it. The rest was just life happening.

God's Favor on Earth

In Psalm 84:11 it says, "For the Lord God is a sun and shield; The Lord will give grace and glory; No good thing will He withhold from those who walk uprightly."

> *My son, do not forget my law, But let your heart keep my commands; For length of days and long life and peace they will add to you. Let not mercy and truth forsake you; bind them around your neck, write them on the tablet of your heart, and so find favor and high esteem in the sight of God and man. Trust in the Lord with all your heart, and lean not on your own understanding; in all your ways acknowledge Him, and He shall direct your paths. Do not be wise in your own eyes; Fear the Lord and depart from evil. It will break health to your flesh, and strength to your bones. Honor the Lord with your possessions, and with the first fruits of all your increase; so your barns will be filled with plenty, and your vats will overflow with new wine.*
>
> (Proverbs 3:1–10)

When you read the previous scripture, you can see the reward and favor the Lord gives when we honor Him and obey His commands. He tells us that no good thing will be withheld from us (keep in mind, this is according to His will and not just what we want, or think, is good for us). He instructs us to write His commands on our hearts, to tie them around our necks. Think about that. Think about the weight of His commands and what it would be like to tie that yoke around our necks. Think about what that means when we are walking around with the Lord's words in our hearts and around our neck like "dead" weights. But they aren't dead weights; they are "life weights." They bring life as we carry and implement them. And guess what? People who don't even believe in the Lord yet operate in godly principles reap the benefits of those principles, simply because the Lord's word does not return void. It brings health to our flesh and strength to our bones, which leads to a long, peaceful life. He promises abundance of harvest and prosperity. Now, don't confuse this with the prosperity gospel. This is not what that is. The Lord promises prosperity when we obey His commands and fear Him, revere Him. We don't just prosper when we accept salvation, and that's all we have to do. Oh no, we have to die to ourselves, lay our lives down, and take up our cross to follow Him. We have to love others, including our enemies. We should be discipling people and sharing the good news of the cross. There are prerequisites to this prosperity. And it's not easy, but the rewards are great, as you can see. Our families benefit from it, and our lives will directly reflect the reward of honor.

Eternal Rewards

We not only receive the Lord's favor on earth, but we also reap eternal rewards. One thing that can be frustrating, when we focus on our life here on earth, is that we don't always see the reward of honor on earth. I think what is important to remember is that we don't choose to honor people to reap the rewards, we choose to honor them because of our love for God. When we lose focus on God and sharpen the focus on ourselves, we miss out on all the things God has for us here on earth. We were created in the image of God and were called to look more like Christ. The way we do this is by surrendering to God and taking up our cross, following Him. Obedience is what leads us to blessings of the Lord. It is better than what we give up when we die to ourselves. Everything God has is better. Every thought He has, plan He has, and path He has are better than what we could imagine up for ourselves. Why not try to focus on treating others with the utmost respect, regardless of position? Even if we don't reap the rewards here on earth, we most certainly will reap them in Heaven (Matthew 6). Let us sow honor into the lives of those we meet and those we already know. Let's focus on our relationship with Christ, and as we encounter difficulty of honoring someone due to conflict, dislike, or just because we want to be petty in that moment, let us take a moment to remember what Christ did for us, who He is, and who He says we are. It can be a moment-by-moment journey if this is something that you struggle with. Just know that we all struggle. Everyone absolutely struggles because we are human and we are promised trials and hardships. We are promised persecution, so count it all joy, and remember that we can ask the Lord to lead us in all things (James 1:2–7).

If you find yourself in a situation where this is the first time you're learning about honor this way, please know that you can start now. One thing I did for myself and my children, and future generations, was I prayed. I prayed prayers of repentance; I sought out forgiveness for my ancestors who did not believe or walk in the ways of Christ. I offered forgiveness, and I asked the Lord to cleanse and heal *all* areas that came to mind and even those that I couldn't think of. God knows all! I wanted to take accountability on behalf of family members who couldn't, and I wanted to forgive those who may have done things that caused curses to be attached to me and my family. I am honestly willing to pray about absolutely anything, even if it sounds silly. God is omniscient, and I know that I can ask anything, especially wisdom, to ensure that my life is all that it can be while I'm here on earth. This doesn't just apply to what my past family members and parents have done, but also to things that I have done, said, and thought about. He can cleanse and heal it all, and I want to ensure that my children live the life God intended us to live before the Fall of Adam and Eve. Check this out. Are you ready? Seriously, because I have encountered a lot of people who don't actually believe this.

Jesus Christ took on the wrath of God and died for the atonement of our sins—*All our sins. He. Broke. The. Curse!* He broke the curse! He *broke* the curse! Y'all, come on now! Whom the Son sets free is free *INDEED* (John 8:36). We have to believe this. We just have to. There is no excuse. The Cross took care of it all, and if we believe in that, we can truly walk in the full freedom that Christ afforded us. I mean, He took care of it all. I don't know how many times or ways I can say it, but let it sit in your heart, your mind, and your spirit, and trust that God did it all. Just walk in obedience to His word and where He leads you. You can have the joy of the Lord and the peace of the Prince resting in you, even when you walk through trials. I love you and am very thankful that you took the time to read this to the end. I pray this over you today:

> *May the Lord bless you and protect you. May the Lord smile on you and be gracious to you. May the Lord show you his favor and give you his peace.*
>
> (Numbers 6:25–26 NLT)

In Jesus' Name,
Amen.

ENDORSEMENT

"Tiffany is not only gifted, she is passionate. She's a worshipper at her core and has been intentional about glorifying God in all she does. She's authentic and humble and her story will bless you."

JADA EDWARDS, BIBLE TEACHER,
WORSHIP PASTOR, AUTHOR.

"In life, there are times when God allows us to meet people who are the actual embodiment of Christ's love. I've had the great pleasure of knowing Mrs. Tiffany Graham since she was a high school student in San Antonio, Texas. I have watched Tiffany evolve from a young, disengaged teenager, who consistently dined at the table of worldly popularity, to a powerful purveyor of God's grace and love.

I have seen the many opportunities for her to use her unparalleled voice for personal gain, but like many before her in the faith, decided to use her talents to glorify God.

When we peruse the vicissitudes of her life, we will undoubtedly see how she has relied, not on her personal gifts and abilities, but God's grace. We will readily notice the times when she doubted herself and her mission, only later to be engulfed in the mission of God.

Her Master's in Counseling gives her some of the empirical and anecdotal messaging that can help the masses overcome their situations; but it's her authentic relationship with God that gives the masses HOPE! Hope in a power that supersedes degrees, accolades, and every trapping of this world.

I can unequivocally and irrefutably say, Mrs. Tiffany Graham's book will give you the blueprint to unleash those impediments stifling your spiritual, natural, and professional growth. Her words will challenge you to pursue God's will for your life. They will bring meaning to the trials that you have faced and usher you in the presence of an Almighty God that heals the broken hearted, sets the captives free, and gives us a mission to make an indelible, and intergenerational impact on this world for the Kingdom's Sake."

Dr. Lawrence Scott
Associate Professor, TAMUSA
College of Education and Human Development
Department of Educator and Leadership Preparation

About the Book

The Honoring Life is a spiritual empowerment book intended for women who come from broken or dysfunctional backgrounds and struggle with honoring people in positions of authority/leadership due to lack of trust in God. Topics on honor, and how to apply it in everyday life, will include marriage, parents, community leaders (pastors, law enforcement, politicians, etc.), and most importantly God. Journal pages are included at the end of certain chapters so readers can take notes or journal their thoughts and action steps after reading. I believe this book is necessary for a time such as this because there is a lack of honor in various areas when it comes to relationships. Honor towards God, in marriage, for community leaders and law enforcement, and pastors seems to be a lost virtue. Not to mention the lack of honor for others in general. This is especially true in our community today where there is an excessive amount of social unrest and lack of regard for life. As women learn to honor using biblical principles, their character will be reflected within their actions and will ultimately pour out as influence into their immediate relationships, causing a shift in their environment, and producing good fruit that flows from heaven. It is a necessary topic, especially for women, because there are limited books that speak on honor in the way that *The Honoring Life* will. Please note that men can benefit from the words in this book as well, but the intended audience is meant for women.

Printed in the USA
CPSIA information can be obtained
at www.ICGtesting.com
JSHW011754240923
48796JS00011B/293